# PSALMS
# FOR THE
# ANXIOUS HEART

## A 30-DAY DEVOTIONAL
## FOR UNCERTAIN TIMES

# BECKY HARLING

MOODY PUBLISHERS
CHICAGO

All Scripture quotations, unless otherwise indicated, are taken from the Holy Bible, New International Version®, NIV®. Copyright © 1973, 1978, 1984, 2011 by Biblica, Inc.™ Used by permission of Zondervan. All rights reserved worldwide. www.zondervan .com. The "NIV" and "New International Version" are trademarks registered in the United States Patent and Trademark Office by Biblica, Inc.™

Scripture quotations marked NLT are taken from the Holy Bible, New Living Translation, copyright ©1996, 2004, 2015 by Tyndale House Foundation. Used by permission of Tyndale House Publishers, Inc., Carol Stream, Illinois 60188. All rights reserved.

Scripture quotations marked PHILLIPS are taken from The New Testament in Modern English by J.B Phillips, copyright © 1960, 1972 J. B. Phillips. Administered by The Archbishops' Council of the Church of England. Used by Permission.

All emphasis in Scripture has been added.

Published in association with the literary agency of The Blythe Daniel Agency, Inc., P.O. Box 64197, Colorado Springs, CO 80962-4197.

Edited by Amanda Cleary Eastep
Interior and cover design: Erik M. Peterson
Cover illustration of oil painting copyright © 2019 by SantaLiza / Shutterstock (1148931977). All rights reserved.

All websites and phone numbers listed herein are accurate at the time of publication but may change in the future or cease to exist. The listing of website references and resources does not imply publisher endorsement of the site's entire contents. Groups and organizations are listed for informational purposes, and listing does not imply publisher endorsement of their activities.

Library of Congress Control Number: 2020939041

ISBN: 978-0-8024-2338-2

Originally delivered by fleets of horse-drawn wagons, the affordable paperbacks from D. L. Moody's publishing house resourced the church and served everyday people. Now, after more than 125 years of publishing and ministry, Moody Publishers' mission remains the same—even if our delivery systems have changed a bit. For more information on other books (and resources) created from a biblical perspective, go to: www .moodypublishers.com or write to:

Moody Publishers
820 N. LaSalle Boulevard
Chicago, IL 60610

1 3 5 7 9 10 8 6 4 2

Printed in the United States of America

This book is lovingly dedicated to
my precious and beautiful daughter, Keri Joy Denison.
Keri, from the time you were tiny,
you've been singing praises to God.
I remember tucking you in bed at night
when you were just a toddler.
As I went down the hall, I could hear you singing,
"Lord, you are more precious than silver."
You're an extraordinary worship leader
who leads others passionately into the presence of God.
You have truly learned how
to turn your panic into praise.
Your worship life inspires me!
I am so very proud of you and love you so dearly.

# TURN YOUR PANIC INTO PRAISE

As I write this, the two most popular words on the evening news are "unprecedented and uncertain." The COVID-19 (coronavirus) pandemic has basically ravaged the globe. As the virus has spread worldwide, hundreds of thousands of people have died, and the global economy is teetering on the brink of disaster. Lovely, hey? This pandemic will be recorded in future history books, and it will leave an indelible imprint on all of our lives. Mental health issues such as anxiety and depression are on the rise more than ever. And many are predicting that vast numbers of people will deal with PTSD after it's all over.

I am no stranger to anxiety. I feel like I've battled worry and fear since childhood. That's why I've written this book.

I wanted to give you a resource—a battle plan—that you could use as you fight worry, fear, and discouragement.

Since my college years, I've read the Psalms every day as a part of my early morning times with Jesus. I have found comfort and friendship for my soul in the words of the psalmists. They, like me, wrestled with worry, fear, doubt, and discouragement. Yet, after they poured out their hearts to the Lord, they proceeded to praise Him. As they praised God, their souls were transformed. Oh, these Psalms have become precious to me!

I first learned the extraordinary power of praise while battling breast cancer. With the looming threat of surgery, fears of death, worries about my kids, and generalized feelings of anxiety, I hardly felt like jumping up and down and shouting "Hallelujah!" Yet, I began to intentionally practice praising God every morning. Sometimes, my worship was simply weeping at His feet.

As I faithfully praised God, I began to notice changes. Fear was transformed into courage, doubt to faith, and anxiety to peace. Authentically speaking, does this mean I never feel anxious anymore? Or that I never worry or feel afraid anymore? No. What it means is I now have a plan when I feel overwhelmed. **I turn my panic into**

**praise.** Honestly, I've written this book during a time in my life where panic has threatened again. Between the COVID-19 crisis and a job change for my husband, anxiety could have overwhelmed me. Each time I've felt anxiety rising, I shifted my focus to the Almighty One who loves and provides.

Friend, I don't know what challenges you are facing at this moment in your personal history. Perhaps you've lost a job and are wondering about your financial livelihood; perhaps you're wrestling with physical or mental health issues. Maybe overall you're doing okay, but underneath, there's an undercurrent of anxiety about the future. Here's what I can promise you: if you will cultivate the practice of praising and worshiping God every day, He will speak peace into your storm. It may take a while, but if you will persist, you will experience calm like the person written about in Jeremiah 17:7–8:

> But blessed is the one who trusts in the LORD,
>      whose confidence is in him.
> They will be like a tree planted by the water
>      that sends out its roots by the stream.
> It does not fear when heat comes:
>      its leaves are always green.

It has no worries in a year of drought
and never fails to bear fruit.

The change will be gradual, but the blessing of His presence during your times with Him will be immediate. You will begin to experience His love in ways you never imagined.

So where do we go from here?

Each day of this devotional includes:

**A Verse or Two from the Psalms.** During seasons of difficulty, less is often better than more. Meditating on just a bite-size portion of Scripture will help you focus your thoughts intentionally.

**A Devotional Thought.** After each Scripture, there is a short devotional with reflections on the Scriptures and what those Scriptures speak about anxiety, fear, loneliness, or discouragement.

**Selah—Pause and Reflect.** In this section, you will stop and consider a question. These questions are designed to help you think. Through the Psalms, you will see the word "selah" often. This Hebrew word basically means: Stop. Pause. Reflect on what you've just read. The practice of pausing will allow you to reflect and consider what God is speaking to you. Please don't rush through. Instead, take a few moments to consider. Ask the Holy Spirit to awaken your heart to what He wants you to know from His Word.

**Today's Truth.** It is helpful during difficult seasons to consider one truth from each Scripture. These truths will be a key to setting you free from anxiety.

**Listen.** Each day, I will suggest a worship song to listen to on your preferred music platform. Allow the music to prompt your praise. If you are physically able, get on your knees as you listen. Please understand, my music tastes may not be yours. You could easily choose your own music style of worship songs and create your own worship playlist. In any case, worship music is designed to help prompt our praise. For easy reference, the songs are listed in the back of the book too.

**Pray.** Finally, there is a sample scriptural prayer at the end of each day. Many of these prayers came right out of my own prayer journal. They are included to show you the power of praying Scripture to free you from anxiety.

As you pray these prayers and faithfully praise God, I believe you will gradually find freedom from much of your anxiety. Having said that, if you are taking medicine under the direction of a doctor for anxiety or depression, please continue. In addition, getting enough sleep and regularly exercising are very beneficial when wrestling anxiety.

Friend, please know that as you take this 30-day journey, I'll be praying for you. I know the battle with anxiety all too well. I pray this will be a life-changing journey for you. I'm cheering for you, and, even better, Jesus Himself is cheering you on!

> May God's peace calm your anxious heart,
> Becky

*But you, LORD,*
*are a shield around me,*
*my glory, the One who lifts*
*my head high.*

PSALM 3:3

I remember lying in bed one night long ago, unable to sleep. Uncertainty gripped my heart with fingers of fear, strangling out all rational thought. I was teetering on the brink of a full-blown panic attack. I wanted to trust God. I just wasn't sure I could get my heart there. Can you relate? Ever had a panic attack? Life can, at times, hurl at us the unexpected and leave us shaken to the core.

When David wrote Psalm 3, he was shaken to the core. He was on the run from his son Absalom who was trying to kill him and overtake the throne. I can't imagine one of my kids being so angry that they wanted to kill me, can you? David poured out his heart to the Lord but then made this glorious proclamation about God being his shield.

The apostle Paul also mentions a shield in his famous passage on the armor of God in Ephesians 6. He calls it the shield of faith. In both passages, the shield is God's faithfulness. We don't create a shield by conjuring up enough faith. When uncertainty, fear, and anxiety pummel our minds, we often can't come up with what we feel is enough faith.

The great reassurance from this passage is that you don't have to. Simply put your faith—however small—in the person of Christ Jesus. His very nature is faithfulness. He is the one who shields our thinking in the day of battle. When we focus on His faithful goodness, the Holy Spirit shields our minds from the tormenting attacks of the enemy. God's faithfulness literally becomes a shield around our minds, but only as we choose to focus our thoughts on Him.

Today, when fear threatens to capture your thinking, take those thoughts prisoner. Shift your focus to praising God. He is your shield. His faithfulness will guard your thinking as you fix your thoughts on Him.

**Selah—Pause and Reflect:** *What reminders do you have of God's faithfulness in the past that might prompt you to trust Him today?*

**Today's Truth:** *In times of uncertainty and fear, fix your thoughts on God's faithfulness.*

**Listen:** *"I Will Praise You" sung by Hillsong Worship and "Take Courage" sung by Kristene DiMarco*

**Pray:** Lord Jesus, in these uncertain days, I often feel anxious and afraid. I bow before You and praise You for Your unfailing love in my life. I take the shield of Your faithfulness, and I hold it up against any attack of the enemy toward my mind. I praise You that I can trust You to accomplish what concerns me. Lord God, Your Word teaches me that the key to keeping my mind at peace is to focus my thoughts on You. Holy One, You have already established peace for me. You are good, holy, faithful, and true. You alone are worthy of all my praise. You are worthy, Lord, to receive glory and honor and power.

*(Psalm 138:8; Isaiah 26:3, 12–13; Ephesians 6:16; Revelation 4:11)*

*Many, LORD, are asking,*
*"Who will bring us prosperity?"*
*Let the light of your face shine on us.*

PSALM 4:6

David, the writer of this psalm, gives voice to several of the fears that pummel our hearts in the face of a crisis. It almost feels as if he is living through our current pandemic. David writes, "Many, LORD, are asking, 'who will bring us prosperity?'" In other words, "Where is our provision?"

When the children of Israel wandered through the desert, they complained about their lack. Lack of proper food, lack of water, and lack of direction (Ex. 16). God provided manna for them to eat each day. The Israelites asked, "What is it?" And that's where the name manna came from (v. 31). They could only gather enough for that day. If they tried to collect more, it became rotten. This became a test of their faith. Would they trust God to provide for each day? God led them through the wilderness with the cloud of His presence during the day and the fire of His presence at night. As David writes this psalm, he remembers it is the light of God's presence that provides for our lack as we journey through the wilderness.

Friend, in times of crisis, it's easy to focus on what we lack. Feeling fearful, we look at the stock market and wonder, will it crash? Will we have a job? Will we be able to make our house payment? So many questions.

In the exact moment of our panic, we need to turn our eyes toward the light of His presence and remember He Himself is our provision. His nature lacks nothing! He is the glorious, eternal one who is our Creator, Provider, Healer, and Sustainer. He does not lack and promises that, even in the wilderness, He Himself will be our provision.

**Selah—Pause and Reflect:** *When you feel panic hit, where do you most often run? Netflix, food, alcohol? What does it look like for you to focus your attention on the God who lacks nothing and who promises to be your provision?*

**Today's Truth:** *He Himself is your provision.*

**Listen:** *"With You" sung by Elevation Worship*

**Pray:** Lord God, the Almighty One, I praise You that You are the glorious one who lacks nothing. Let the light of Your face shine on me. Remind me that You are the all-sustaining Creator. You are the glorious one who lacks nothing. Open my eyes to see Your provision and presence more clearly. Strengthen me to trust You more completely. I praise You that through You, all things were created and that in everything, You have preeminence. I praise You that You are the God who is completely self-sustaining. Certainly I can trust You even when I don't understand. I praise You that there is no need that I have that You cannot fill. Your glorious nature is able to provide all that I need. Thank You that I can lie down and rest in complete peace, trusting Your glorious nature to provide and protect while I sleep.

*(Colossians 1:17; Psalm 4:6, 8; 23:1)*

*In the morning, LORD,*
*you hear my voice;*
*in the morning*
*I lay my requests before you*
*and wait expectantly.*

PSALM 5:3

Everything seems to come to a screeching halt in the face of crisis. During the COVID-19 crisis, everything has stopped: businesses shuttered, schools closed, church services cancelled. The world seems to have stopped, quite literally, on its axis. The uncertainty has left many feeling uneasy and insecure, and asking, "Where is God in this mess? Has He forgotten us?"

Friend, God has not forgotten you. Where is He? He is listening. He hears the cries of your heart and the faintest whispers of your longings. The psalmist, David, cries out to God, "Hear my cry for help, my King and my God, for to you I pray" (Ps. 5:2). Then David goes on to write these profound words of hope: "In the morning, LORD, you hear my voice; in the morning I lay my requests before you and wait expectantly" (v. 3). What helped David shift his prayer from a desperate plea to a prayer of hope? I believe it was because of the personal understanding David had of God's character. In tender affection, David calls God *my* king and *my* God.

Friend, though God is infinitely vast and beyond our wildest imagination, He is intimately personal. When *you* cry, He hears and bends down to listen as a loving Father (Ps. 116:2 NLT). The writer of Hebrews confirms this truth, instructing us to come confidently into the throne room with our requests. There, in His loving presence, we will find grace for our every need (Heb. 4:16). Today, lay your requests before Him, and wait with anticipation for His answer.

**Selah—Pause and Reflect:** *What are the longings of your heart in this moment? What does it look like to lay those desires confidently before the Lord and wait with hope for Him to answer?*

**Today's Truth:** *God is a God who listens to every whisper of your soul. Trust He is listening today, and lay your requests boldly before Him.*

**Listen:** *"Just Want You" sung by Sarah Reeves and The Belonging Co*

**Pray:** Lord, I praise You because You are my King and my God. Though You are the King of the universe, You are a loving Father to me. While You are infinite beyond my wildest imagination, You are intimately acquainted with every tiny detail of my life. I praise You that I can boldly come into Your throne room and lay every request—both big and small—at Your feet. Thank You, Lord Jesus, that You told me I could ask You for anything and that I should keep on asking until You answer. Lord, in the moments when You seem silent and my heart is tempted to believe You don't care or that You have forgotten me, strengthen my resolve to keep asking. Help me to hold on to the promise that You are listening and that You will respond according to Your will. I believe You, Lord; strengthen me in my moments of unbelief. I praise You in advance for how You will work in each situation that I have laid at Your feet. I praise You that I can trust You.

*(Psalm 5:2; Hebrews 4:16; Matthew 7:7; Mark 9:24)*

*Those who know
your name trust in you,
for you, LORD,
have never forsaken
those who seek you.*

PSALM 9:10

We were designed for community. Created in the image of a relational God, our hearts crave connection. When deep bonds are missing, we panic. As I write this, the coronavirus pandemic is raging and has raised our feelings of panic. With both voluntary and state-mandated social distancing, many are feeling isolated and lonely. Even though we try to stay connected through social media and online video calls, it's not the same. We miss authentic, in-person community.

The psalmist David had his lonely moments as well. Isolated and running from King Saul, David had reason to feel lonely. Yet David wrote these profound words to address our loneliness: "For you, LORD, have never forsaken those who seek you" (Ps. 9:10). The writer of Hebrews echoes this truth and reminds us that God says, "Never will I leave you; never will I forsake you" (Heb. 13:5).

Friend, as you read this, you might be suffering and feeling isolated. You might be grieving the loss of a loved one, job, security, or home and feel like you have no one who understands. I have good news for you: you are not alone! Our Savior came into our sorrow and suffering, and He has promised that He will never leave us—no matter what comes our way. He understands the grief in your heart and the sorrow in your soul. You are not alone. He is with you. You have a 24/7 companion through the trials of life.

**Selah—Pause and Reflect:** *How do you best experience the presence of Christ? Who are three people you could call in a crisis who would support you and strengthen you?*

**Today's Truth:** *You are never alone. God's presence goes before, behind, above, and beneath you. He will never leave you nor forsake you.*

**Listen:** *"Isn't He" sung by Natalie Grant and The Belonging Co*

**Pray:** Lord Jesus, I praise You that You have promised You will never leave me nor forsake me. Thank You that Your presence is continually with me. If I go up to the highest heavens or down to the darkest place of the deep, You are there. You hold my hand as I journey through life. When I feel lost, You guide me. When I feel afraid, You comfort me. Your love holds me secure. Nothing I do can separate me from Your eternal affection. Even if others abandon me, You will not. I praise You that even in the darkness of life's wilderness, Your presence is with me. Thank You for the empathy You offer me when I am grieving. You weep with me in my sorrow and rejoice with me in my triumph! Thank You that You have called me to be Your friend. Not only do You call me Your friend, but You graciously give me those whom I can call friends. Thank You specifically for

_____ [write

in the names of three friends to whom You are close that You can turn to when discouraged]. I praise and exalt You for designing me for community and for modeling friendship for me. I exalt You, Lord Jesus!

*(Psalm 27:10; 73:23–24; 139:7–10; Romans 8:35; John 11:36; 15:14)*

*Why, LORD, do you stand far off?*
*Why do you hide yourself*
*in times of trouble?*

PSALM 10:1

Questions. We all have them when trouble and trials hit. We wonder, "Where are you, God?" And perhaps more profound, "Why aren't you stepping in to do something?" After all, God is all-powerful, all-loving and all-sovereign. In our humanity we wonder why God doesn't do something when it feels like the whole world is falling apart.

We are not alone in our questioning. For thousands of years, great and godly people have sobbed from the pit of despair, "Why?" When God allowed Satan to mess with Job, stripping him bare of all that was precious to him, Job cried out, "Therefore I will not keep silent; I will speak out in the anguish of my spirit, I will complain in the bitterness of my soul" (Job 7:11). He goes on to cry, "I desire to speak to the Almighty and to argue my case with God" (13:3).

David cried out in anguish, "Why, LORD, do you stand far off? Why do you hide yourself in times of trouble?" (Ps. 10:1). Wait. Are we allowed to argue with God? Are we allowed to cry out in our anguish and ask why? The answer to that lies in the cross of Christ where, in utter torment and agony, Jesus cried out, "My God, my God, why have you forsaken me?" (Matt. 27:46).

Prayers of lament are an integral part of our spiritual journey. A lament is when we wrestle our sorrow out with God, but in the end, we bow before Him in worship, acknowledging He is sovereign and we are not. In the end, Job worshiped God and said, "I know that you can do all things; no purpose of yours can be thwarted." He goes on to say, "My ears had heard of you but now my eyes have seen you" (Job 42:2, 5). David finishes his lament by bowing in worship, saying, "The LORD is King for ever and ever" (Ps. 10:16). Jesus laments in the garden and on the cross, but bows to the Father's will (Luke 22:42).

Ah, friend, the sacred language of lament is a part of our deep worship of God. The key is to turn toward God in your questioning rather than away from Him. Cry it out in the arms of the Almighty, and there you will experience the merciful lovingkindness of God.

**Selah—Pause and Reflect:** *When have you used the language of lament in your times of prayer with God? Did you feel guilty after? How might you experience the deep love of God by being more authentic in your prayer times?*

**Today's Truth:** *In your times of questioning and sorrow, turn toward God rather than away from Him.*

**Listen:** *"I Know" sung by Big Daddy Weave*

**Pray:** Oh, Lord Jesus, I have so many questions. So often when I see suffering and hardship all around me, my soul screams, "Why?" My mind wonders, "Why don't You step in and do something?" Yet, I know that You are God, and I am not. Oh, Lord, I want to trust You, and most of the time I do, but with all the suffering around me, I feel my faith shaken to the core. Strengthen me, I pray. Teach me to bow at Your feet. Thank You that You let me weep and cry in Your presence. You collect all my tears in Your bottle and consider each tear precious. Like a loving Father, You hold me in Your almighty arms and weep with me. I praise You that I don't have a God who can't empathize with me but one who is well-acquainted with sorrow and suffering.

*(Psalm 56:8; Isaiah 53:3; John 11:36; Hebrews 4:15)*

# *How long, LORD?*

## PSALM 13:1

Waiting is the worst. Waiting when you're excited with anticipation is one thing, but waiting for breakthrough when you're in dire circumstances feels horrible. As I write this, we around the globe are asking, "How long, Lord?"

David was well-acquainted with waiting. Anointed by God in his teens to be the next king, David had to wait years before the fulfillment of God's promise.

Though we hate waiting, God uses waiting in our lives to sharpen us as His servants and set the stage for His will. As the Alpha and the Omega (Rev. 1:8), He holds time and eternity in His hands. His perspective on timing is vastly different from ours. We are usually in a rush, right? God uses delay to sharpen us and set the stage for how He wants to use us. Yet, in our humanity, we long for Him to hurry up. As we wait for Him and lean into His refining process rather than pulling away, the Holy Spirit transforms us. We are shaped into someone who looks a whole lot more like Jesus. Often it is only in the crucible of waiting that we emerge radiating the fruit of His Spirit: love, joy, peace, and patience.

Rather than asking, "How long, LORD?" perhaps a better question might be, "How can I cooperate with what You're doing in my life right now?" Only those who have been in the fire of the crucible of waiting are able to emerge as the polished instruments of God.

**Selah—Pause and Reflect:** *How has God used seasons of waiting in your life in the past? What lessons did you learn during that season that might otherwise not have been learned?*

**Today's Truth:** *God uses waiting to sharpen you as His instrument and to set the stage for what He's called you to do.*

**Listen:** *"Be Strong" sung by Jon Egan*

**Pray:** Oh, Lord, I hate waiting! I realize just how impatient I am when I compare myself with You. I feel like I'm hopelessly addicted to hurry. Oh, Holy Spirit, change me. I pray that You will create in me a quiet heart. One that waits with holy trust in Your character. Teach me to be like Jesus. I praise You, Lord Jesus, that You are the Alpha and the Omega, the one who is, and who was, and who is to come! I praise You that You see the entire landscape of eternity. You are worthy to govern the universe because You have conquered sin and death and hell. Now You live forever seated at the right hand of Father God. My heart cries "Holy, Holy, Holy is the Lord God Almighty." Thank you that even though You are never in a rush, Your timing is always perfect. I praise You that while I wait, I can trust Your unfailing love, and my heart can rejoice that You are working even when I can't see that. I praise You that You have been good to me and that Your plans for me are good.

*(Psalm 13:5–6; Jeremiah 29:11; Revelation 1:8; 4:8)*

*I love you, LORD, my strength.*
*The LORD is my rock,*
*my fortress and my deliverer;*
*my God is my rock,*
*in whom I take refuge,*
*my shield and the horn of my salvation,*
*my stronghold.*

PSALM 18:1–2

My husband, Steve, and I like to hike. One of the most intriguing things about Colorado where we live is the beautiful rock formations. The Garden of the Gods is one of the most beautiful parks in the world. The red rocks are spectacular and breathtaking. When we take our little grandsons hiking with us, they like to scramble and hide in the different crevices of the majestic rocks. There, hidden in the rocks, they have their own fortress.

When troubles and trials upend our lives, we long for a hiding place. David was well-acquainted with hiding places. He often hid in caves while running from King Saul (1 Sam. 22:1). In Psalm 18, David gives us several beautiful metaphors for the Lord as our hiding place. The metaphors David uses to describe his relationship with the Lord are the same metaphors you can use when you feel stressed or anxious.

Close your eyes for just a moment. Imagine, God Himself is *your* rock, *your* fortress, *your* deliverer, and *your* refuge. He shelters you with His presence when you are surrounded by fear and anxiety. He shields your mind in the day of battle. Keep your thoughts sheltered in His presence. His presence is what calms our fears.

**Selah—Pause and Reflect:** *What does it look like for you to hide in God's presence today?*

**Today's Truth:** *God is our hiding place in times of trouble.*

**Listen:** *"Hiding Place" sung by All Peoples Worship, featuring Keri Denison (by the way, Keri is my daughter!)*

**Pray:** Lord Jesus, I love You. You are my Strength, my Rock, my Refuge, my Hiding Place, and my Fortress. When fear and anxiety surround me, You are my Deliverer. I pray that the brightness of Your presence would surround and envelop me today. Help me to remember in these uncertain times that nothing catches You by surprise. When I feel like I'm drowning in anxiety, You will reach down with Your almighty hand and rescue me from the enemy. I praise You that though I don't know what the future looks like, You turn my darkness into light, and with Your help I can scale any seemingly impossible wall because You are with me. I praise You that You arm me with strength, and You hide me within the shelter of Your presence. Remind me through my day that the Lord lives! Praise be to my Rock! Exalted are You God, my Savior!

*(Psalm 18:1–2, 16, 28–29, 32, 46)*

*May these words of my mouth
and this meditation of my heart
be pleasing in your sight,
LORD, my Rock and my Redeemer.*

PSALM 19:14

Our words matter. Author Dallas Willard wrote, "The first act of faith is to speak."[1] Often when surrounded by trouble, we are fearful that we lack enough faith for God to move. However, this is the exact moment when we need to speak faith into our circumstances.

I love the story found in Mark 9 where a father comes to Jesus asking Him to heal his son. The father is distraught. Who could blame him? His son has been terrorized by a demon since he was small. The demon would often throw the boy "into fire or water to kill him." Talk about stress! The father is panicked. Jesus is his last resort. He begs Jesus, "If you can do anything, take pity on us and help us." Jesus responds lovingly, "'If you can?' Everything is possible for one who believes." The poor father is likely weeping at this point and whimpers, "I do believe; help me overcome my unbelief!" (Mark 9:21–24).

When we feel we don't have enough faith, we can sink to scolding or shaming ourselves for our lack of faith. Your words have power. This is why praise is so important. When you feel your faith lacking, simply begin to speak out loud your praises to God. Echo the psalmist's prayer, "May these words of my mouth and this meditation of my heart be pleasing in your sight" (Ps. 19:14).

Meditate on His goodness, and praise Him for His character. Change your self-talk and the words you speak out loud. In other words, stop using your internal words to shame yourself. Instead, declare out loud your worship of God. As you praise Him, your faith will rise, and Satan, who is the accuser, will flee. Friend, never beat yourself up for not having enough faith. Simply change your language and start using your words to praise God.

**Selah—Pause and Reflect:** *How does Satan use our negative self-talk to torment us and keep us in a cesspool of shame? How does praising God lift us up out of the cesspool and set our feet on the Rock?*

**Today's Truth:** *Our words are powerful. Use your mouth to declare God's praise, and your faith will be strengthened.*

**Listen:** *"You Say" sung by Lauren Daigle*

**Pray:** Lord God, I praise You for creating me with the ability to praise You. Thank You that when Satan torments me with self-doubt and shame, I can choose how I will respond. Thank You that when I begin to use my mouth to praise You, Satan flees. Lord, in times of fear and uncertainty, I praise You that You have promised to send me help and grant me strength. I thank You that the extraordinary power of praise is this: as I choose to praise You, Your Holy Spirit strengthens my faith. Lord, grow me into a mature believer whose trust is so rooted in You that when seasons of drought come, I don't give into fear. May the words of my mouth and the focus of my heart exalt You today!

*(Psalm 19:14; Jeremiah 17:7–8)*

*Guide me in your truth
and teach me,
for you are God my Savior,
and my hope is in you all day long.*

PSALM 25:5

Uncertainty. Just the word stirs up fear. We can cope with almost anything if we know what's coming and can get mentally prepared, right? But what about seasons when we are left in the dark and haven't a clue about what will happen next? Ah, that's when panic sets in.

David wrote out his prayer song, "Guide me in your truth and teach me, for you are God my Savior, and my hope is in you all day long" (Ps. 25:5). The Hebrew word used here for *truth* means, "certainty, stability, truth, rightness."[2] Life felt very uncertain to David. He cries out for Yahweh to guide him, and he's looking for certainty.

David then continues by writing, "My hope is in you." The Hebrew word that is translated *hope* here carries the idea of being bound together with the Lord. It reminds me of Abigail's words to David when he was angry and threatening to kill everyone in the household of Nabal: "Even when you are chased by those who seek to kill you you, your life is safe in the care of the LORD your God, secure in his treasure pouch" (1 Sam. 25:29 NLT). Friend, even when life feels uncertain, you are safe in the care of the Lord, securely held in His treasure pouch. That is where your hope lies. Nurture your hope by staying aware of His presence through your day.

**Selah—Pause and Reflect:** *When life feels uncertain, how can you stay aware of the Lord's presence and remember that you are bound to Him?*

**Today's Truth:** *When times are uncertain, remember you have a very sure hope. You are intrinsically connected to God, safe and secure in His treasure pouch.*

**Listen:** *"In Christ Alone" sung by Geoff Moore and The Distance*

**Pray:** Holy One, my hope is in You. How I praise You that You hold me secure in Your treasure pouch when life feels turned upside down. I praise You that I can trust You to guide me step-by-step even when life feels dark. Thank You for the promise that those who hope in the Lord will renew their strength and soar like an eagle. I praise You, Lord, that You are good and have abundant good things in store for me as I consistently nurture my trust in You. I praise You that You will strengthen me day by day through these uncertain days. Thank You for the promise to instruct me and teach me the way to go even during uncertain days.

*(1 Samuel 25:29; Psalm 31:19, 24; 32:8; Isaiah 40:31)*

*The LORD is close
to the brokenhearted
and saves those
who are crushed in spirit.*

PSALM 34:18

Grieving has an honored place in our spiritual jour-neys. Often, we make the mistake of thinking that our Christian walk should be all "happy-clappy" when in reality, Jesus was a Man of Sorrows who said, "Blessed are those who mourn, for they will be comforted" (Matt. 5:4).

God invites us to feel all of our emotions. Jesus Him-self "offered up prayers and petitions with fervent cries and tears" (Heb. 5:7). Friend, when life is falling apart, it's okay to cry. We tend to exalt being strong and being happy emotionally as the trophy of Christian maturity. God, however, calls us to authentically embrace all the emotions. Grieving allows the cleansing of our heart's wounds. If we don't grieve, those wounds become infected and we become bitter. David writes, under the inspiration of the Spirit, "The LORD is close to the brokenhearted and saves those who are crushed in spirit" (Ps. 34:18).

As long as we live on earth, suffering and sorrow will be a part of our journey. Unless we embrace grieving as a spiritual discipline, we won't be able to grow through our suffering and reach a more complete maturity in Christ. Our hope comes from the promise that while we grieve, the Lord Himself comes close and comforts us. Without our seasons of grieving, perhaps we would never know the Lord as intimately.

**Selah—Pause and Reflect:** *What messages did you grow up with about crying and being strong? How might God want to rewrite those messages to bring them more in line with His thoughts?*

**Today's Truth:** *Grieving has an honored place in the life of the believer and is a necessary part of our spiritual growth.*

**Listen:** *"Take Over" sung by Shane & Shane*

**Pray:** Father God, I admit that at times, I prefer to ignore or run from my sorrow and pain. Honestly, thinking about my losses makes me anxious. Rather than facing it, I numb my pain with movies, chocolate cake, social media, or _____ [write in the blank something you commonly run to in order to numb your pain]. Yet, I know that You are inviting me into deeper vulnerability as I journey through grief. Help me to authentically grieve the losses in my life, looking to You as my hope and the one who brings comfort. I praise You because You are the holy one who both weeps with me and comforts me. When I am broken, You speak tenderly to me.

*(Psalm 34:18; Isaiah 40:1–2; John 11:36)*

*I waited patiently for the LORD;*
*he turned to me and heard my cry.*
*He lifted me out of the slimy pit,*
*out of the mud and mire;*
*he set my feet on a rock*
*and gave me a firm place to stand.*
*He put a new song in my mouth,*
*a hymn of praise to our God.*

PSALM 40:1–3a

Discouragement can feel like a muddy pit. In those moments of disappointment and darkness, we feel our attitudes sinking. We can't climb out of the pit like some athletic ninja. With our skill and strength gone, we can only whisper, "Help, God! I need you."

The amazing thing about our God is that short prayers are fine with Him. Think about Peter: when he was walking on the water and started to sink, he simply prayed, "Lord, save me!" (Matt. 14:30). If you remember the story, Jesus stretched out His almighty hand and drew Peter back up from sinking. He does the same with you and me. In those moments when we feel like we're sinking and our only worship is a simple cry for help, Jesus reaches out His hand and pulls us up out of the pit. He sets our feet on a solid foundation once again and puts a new song of praise in our mouths.

Ah, it's a different kind of song. It's no longer just a rote song that we sing by memory in church. No, it's a fresh song of victory because we know it to be true. We remember how dark the pit was, and we are filled with renewed praise at God's goodness in rescuing us. Often the deeper and darker the pit, the deeper and more determined our praise for the one who pulled us out. Then, we bow in worship and echo David's song, singing with renewed determination and admiration, "I desire to do your will, my God" (Ps. 40:8).

**Selah—Pause and Reflect:** *When has God pulled you from the pit of discouragement? How has that renewed your worship of Him?*

**Today's Truth:** *When we've experienced the darkness of the pit, we worship the one who pulled us out with deeper fervency and reverence.*

**Listen:** "Oh Praise the Name" sung by Hillsong Worship

**Pray:** Holy, Merciful Lord, because of Your great love, I am not consumed with discouragement. Your mercies are new every morning, and Your faithfulness is great. I praise You, Lord, that though the pit of discouragement is deep, the depth of Your love is deeper. I praise You for how wide and long and deep and high Your love is for me. I pray that I would know and experience this love even during times of discouragement. Help me remember that You have promised to do more than all I can ask or imagine. I praise You because You heard my cries for help, and You rescued me and put a new song in my mouth—a song of praise to You, God, my King!

*(Psalm 28:6; 40:1–2; Lamentations 3:22–25; Ephesians 3:17–20)*

*Deep calls to deep*
*in the roar of your waterfalls;*
*all your waves and breakers*
*have swept over me.*
*By day the LORD directs his love,*
*at night his song is with me—*
*a prayer to the God of my life.*

PSALM 42:7–8

As a kid, I used to love swimming in the ocean. I loved the thrill of the waves. But I distinctly remember at one point, I feared I was going to drown. While being tossed and turned in the angry surf, I came up gasping for breath only to be sucked back down under the waves. This is the way the psalmist felt in his suffering as he wrote Psalm 42.

Though sung by the sons of Korah, we're not sure who wrote the words. But one thing is clear: the psalmist felt as though all the breakers of life were pummeling him under an angry surf.

Often in seasons of suffering, our minds are pounded with anxious thoughts, and we are left feeling as though we are being tossed and thrown in tumultuous waves. "What ifs" and "what thens" leave our minds churning like a stormy sea. In the turmoil of anxiety and fear, it's difficult to grasp faith. The psalmist clings to the truth that God's love is directed toward him during the day and in the night the Lord gives him a song. Ah, friend, this is the key: *turn your panic into praise.* This is the only way to calm the chaos.

Just as Jesus stood in the boat with His anxious disciples, the storm raging all around, He still speaks today, "Quiet! Be still!" (Mark 4:39). His power and presence will still calm your fears. In the words of author Peter Scazzero, "Courage is not the absence of fear but rather the capacity to step over our fears."[3] When you speak the name of Jesus, you step past your fear. When you speak

His name, the winds and the waves quiet down. When you speak His name, Satan flees. When you speak His name, anxiety bows to the Almighty. Because, friend, His name is the name above every other name!

**Selah—Pause and Reflect:** *Come up with a plan for the next time anxiety attacks your mind. Create a list of ten names of Jesus that you can praise your way through to calm fear (e.g.—Jesus, You are the Prince of Peace).*

**Today's Truth:** *Even when the waves of anxiety are crashing over you, His name still brings peace.*

**Listen:** *"What a Beautiful Name" sung by Brooke Fraser Ligertwood and Hillsong Worship*

**Pray:** Lord Jesus, You are my living God. I thirst for You during this season of difficulty. Honestly, at times I feel like the waves of the ocean are crashing all around me. My mind is churning with anxiety, and I long for peace. I praise You, Lord Jesus, that You are the Prince of Peace. I praise You that You are the Creator of all things. The waves still know Your name. I praise You that Your mere presence and power calm the storm. You promised You would give me peace as I trust in You. As I proclaim Your majesty, I will claim Your promise.

*(Psalm 42:1; Isaiah 9:6; Mark 4:39; John 14:27; Hebrews 12:2)*

*God is our refuge and strength,*
*an ever-present help in trouble.*
*Therefore, we will not fear,*
*though the earth give way*
*and the mountains*
*fall into the heart of the sea.*

PSALM 46:1–2

Right after I was diagnosed with breast cancer, I memorized Psalm 46. With anxiety and fear ravaging my mind, I needed to re-focus my thinking. Every day, leading up to surgery, I walked and repeated the psalm. Those words stayed engraved on my heart and mind. Even now, twenty years later, whenever crisis hits, my mind instantly goes back to Psalm 46. It is a psalm of holy confidence.

God Himself is your refuge. A refuge is a place of shelter and safety. When troubles or trials assault, sending your heart into panic, run to God. Nestle down in His presence as you would a storm cellar during a tornado. He is your all-sufficient strength, your confidence in the face of fear. He is the ever-present One. Ah, I love those words. They still bring peace to my soul. God *never* withdraws Himself from those who are afflicted, anxious, or alarmed. He is closer than your closest friend and more loyal than the most ardent lover. Therefore, you don't have to yield to fear.

Fear can signal danger and help you make wise decisions. But we don't have to be controlled by fear. This is where we learn to "be still and know" that He is God (Ps. 46:10). In the moments when we feel fearful, we can shift our thinking to the Almighty One who is our ever-present help. As we focus on making Him our shelter, He will slow our anxious thoughts and bring us to a place of stillness.

**Selah—Pause and Reflect:** *Imagine God Himself as your refuge and strength. Spend a few moments closing your* *eyes and sitting quietly in His presence. Be still. How does silence and stillness help calm your fear?*

**Today's Truth:** *God is your refuge and strength. Shelter in His presence and be still.*

**Listen:** *"Surrounded" sung by Kari Jobe and "Psalm 46 (Lord of Hosts)" sung by Shane & Shane*

**Pray:** Lord God Almighty, I praise You that You are my refuge and strength. You alone are my confidence in these uncertain days. Even though it seems as though the earth is quaking, You are my place of shelter. I praise You that as I nestle down in Your almighty presence, You bring my anxious thoughts to a halt. Thank You that You will be exalted among the nations. I praise You that one day, every knee will bow and every tongue will confess that You are Lord. You are the Almighty One who rules over all the earth.

*(Psalm 46:1, 10; Romans 14:11)*

*But I am like an olive tree*
*flourishing in the house of God;*
*I trust in God's unfailing love*
*for ever and ever.*
*For what you have done*
*I will always praise you*
*in the presence of your faithful people.*
*And I will hope in your name,*
*for your name is good.*

PSALM 52:8–9

Olive trees are known for their long life. While traveling in Israel several years ago, I visited a garden that had olive trees that were a thousand years old. Those olive trees had definitely flourished. If an olive tree was planted in the temple courts, the psalmist is saying it would have experienced years and years of God's presence.

We are now the temple of God (1 Cor. 6:19). Our bodies house the presence of the living God, the Holy Spirit. We can enjoy God's presence every day and every moment. Though He is with us at all times, when hardship comes, we are tempted to doubt His presence. We might not "feel" His presence, but He is with us. How do we become more aware of His presence moment by moment so that we can flourish even during difficult days?

For years, people have been seeking to experience God's presence more fully. Certainly, there are times in every believer's life when they experience the dark night of the soul. During those seasons, God seems absent.

The question is, how do we flourish and continue to grow in God's presence when life feels dark? There are no easy answers, but since we know that praising God allows us to experience His presence in a deeper way, it's worth doing what the psalmist suggests in Psalm 119:164, "Seven times a day I praise you." Set an alarm on your phone, and stop seven times a day to give God thanks and praise Him for something. As you do this, note if it helps you experience God's presence in a more tangible way.

**Selah—Pause and Reflect:** *How do you best experience God's presence? What fruit might be produced in your life in the more difficult seasons of life?*

**Today's Truth:** *Times of hardship can provide wonderful opportunities to flourish and experience a renewed sense of God's presence.*

**Listen:** *"No One Beside/Have My Heart" sung by Elevation Worship*

**Pray:** Holy One, I praise You that times of difficulty can become fruitful if I keep my focus on enjoying Your presence. Thank You that as I faithfully look to You, Your Holy Spirit will cause fruitfulness in my life. I praise You that You promise that those who remain in You, even during difficult seasons, will flourish and bear much fruit. Oh, Lord, I long to bear much fruit! Thank You that I can trust You to do this in my life!

*(Psalm 52:8–9; 92:12–14; John 15:5)*

*My heart, O God, is steadfast,*
*my heart is steadfast;*
*I will sing and make music.*
*Awake, my soul!*
*Awake, harp and lyre!*
*I will awaken the dawn.*

PSALM 57:7–8

We have steady hearts when circumstances are going well. But the key to a steadfast heart is often the suffering that precedes it as well as the willingness to praise God through it. Certainly, this was true for Corrie ten Boom, a survivor of a Nazi concentration camp.

When Corrie and her sister Betsie first arrived in the

concentration camp, their barrack had fleas. Her sister Betsie told her, "We must give thanks for the fleas." Corrie thought that was ridiculous until she realized that because their barrack had fleas, the guards were afraid to enter. This allowed Betsie and Corrie to have a Bible study in their room every night. Corrie later wrote this after Betsie died and Corrie had been released from the camp: "I would look about as Betsie read, watching the light leap from face to face. More than conquerors . . . . It was not a wish. It was a fact." Corrie continued, "Life in Ravensbruck took place on two separate levels, mutually impossible. One, the observable, external life, grew every day more horrible. The other, the life we lived with God, grew daily better, truth upon truth, glory upon glory."[4]

The apostle Peter certainly didn't always have a steadfast heart. He denied Christ three times right before Jesus was crucified. Yet, after the resurrection and ascension of Christ, we find Peter passionately preaching and writing letters to encourage other believers toward spiritual maturity. He wrote, "And the God of all grace, who called you to his eternal glory in Christ, after you have suffered a little while, will himself restore you and make you strong, firm and steadfast" (1 Peter 5:10). The truth is, suffering leads to a steadfast heart. As we suffer and choose to praise God intentionally through our times of suffering, the Holy Spirit strengthens our hearts in a way that is miraculous.

Friend, are you in a difficult season? Learn to live life on two levels. On one level, life may be terrible. But on another level, you can be enjoying God's goodness. Choose to give thanks and sing. Praise God through the darkness—even though it may not feel authentic. God honors your praise and will strengthen your heart while you worship Him.

**Selah—Pause and Reflect:** *Does it feel authentic to you to praise God when you don't feel like it?*

**Today's Truth:** *Learn to live life on two levels. As you praise God, His Spirit strengthens your heart to be steadfast.*

**Listen:** *"Available" sung by Elevation Worship and "Promises" sung by Maverick City/Tribal*

**Pray:** Lord Jesus, I want a steadfast heart, but truthfully, I don't want to have to go through challenging circumstances to get there. Sigh. Holy Spirit, strengthen my heart to live life on two levels. Help me to understand that while on one level life might feel difficult, on another level, You are strengthening me for the future. Help me to learn to give thanks in all circumstances because I know this is Your will for me.

*(Psalm 57:7–8; 1 Thessalonians 5:17)*

*God will go before me.*

PSALM 59:10

I was a pretty neurotic little kid. I felt anxious about a lot of things, but one of the biggest things I worried about was if I would be strong enough to suffer for Jesus. I know, right? Neurotic. I remember worrying about that as young as ten years old. As I grew in my understanding of God and read His Word faithfully, I gradually began to see that God would go before me. If He called me to suffer, He would provide grace.

Here's the thing. God doesn't seem to dish out grace for suffering beforehand. He goes before us and calls us to trust Him for the things we need. By worrying about tomorrow, or next month, you might be living through nightmares that you were never called to live through.

The psalmist wrote he could rely on God. He trusted God to go before him. In fact, he made it a practice to watch for God's grace (Ps. 59:9–10). Friend, so many of our battles with anxiety, fear, and worry are because we are imagining different scenarios that might never even happen. Be very careful with the stories you tell yourself. Instead of spinning scenarios in your mind, focus your thoughts on Jesus Christ. Pray about your concerns. Pour them out at the feet of Jesus, and then shift your focus to praise and thanksgiving. It takes practice, as the apostle Paul wrote (see Phil. 4:9). However, practice pays off. Gradually, you'll begin to win the war over worry.

The writer of Hebrews reminds us that God gives grace in our hour of need, not necessarily before (Heb. 4:16). Instead of worrying about what might or might not happen tomorrow, rein in your thoughts. Pour out your heart, and then shift your focus to praise. This is the pathway to peace and better mental health.

**Selah—Pause and Reflect:** *How might spinning scenarios about what may or may not happen upend your peace and stir up more anxiety?*

**Today's Truth:** *God gives us grace in our hour of need, not necessarily before. Praise Him that He is reliable and trustworthy.*

**Listen:** *"There Is a King" sung by Elevation Worship*

**Pray:** Lord Jesus, I praise You that You go before me into tomorrow. You've asked me not to worry about my life. Honestly, I confess, this is very hard for me. I want to trust You with tomorrow. Increase my faith to believe that You have everything under control. I lay down every worry and concern at Your feet. I know You have even the hairs of my head numbered and that You love me dearly. When I am tempted to worry, may I focus my attention on what is good, noble, right, pure, lovely, admirable, excellent, and praiseworthy. You alone possess all those character traits. You promise You will provide for my every need according to Your abundance. I trust You, Lord. Holy Spirit, strengthen my heart to trust You even more.

*(Psalm 59:10; Matthew 6:25–27; Philippians 4:8, 19)*

*For you, God, tested us;*
*you refined us like silver.*
*You brought us into prison*
*and laid burdens on our backs.*
*You let people ride over our heads;*
*we went through fire and water,*
*but you brought us*
*to a place of abundance.*

PSALM 66:10–12

One of my favorite quotes from author Ruth Myers is, "Discouragement often precedes enlargement."[5] So extremely simple, yet so profoundly true.

I remember a season in Steve's and my life when we were just starting a new ministry, and a friend gave me these verses. Honestly, at the time, I wanted her to go back and ask the Lord for different verses for me. Who wants to be refined in a furnace or have heavy burdens laid on their backs? Who wants people to ride over their heads, crushing them in a wild stampede? Not me! What about you? Yet, in that season of ministry, that is exactly what happened. We carried huge burdens of illness and other personal issues while people trampled us with criticism. However, God brought us out of that season and into a place of abundant joy and fruitfulness.

The truth is, God often allows deep seasons of discouragement to purify and prepare us for new seasons of fruitfulness, abundance, and impact. Certainly this was true for Joseph. As Daddy's favorite, Joseph was hated by his brothers. It didn't help any that he told them about dreams he had where they were all bowing down to him. You know the rest of the story: sold into slavery, falsely accused, thrown into prison, and forgotten by those who promised to get him out. Joseph had a tough go for years. Yet God was using all those circumstances to shape Joseph into the leader He had called him to be. Eventually, God brought Joseph to the place of abundance and great impact (Gen. 37–50).

Friend, when life is crushing you and you feel like you're in the furnace, praise God that the times of discouragement often precede times of advancement and abundance.

**Selah—Pause and Reflect:** *What are some of the greatest lessons you've learned through seasons of suffering? How might God be shaping you for greater impact through those lessons?*

**Today's Truth:** *Discouragement often precedes enlargement in terms of impact and fruitfulness.*

**Listen:** *"Christ Be Magnified" sung by Cody Carnes*

**Pray:** Lord Jesus, I exalt You! I praise You that though I walk through seasons of discouragement, You can use those seasons to prepare me for what's next. The refining that You allow in my life can shape me for future advancement and impact in Your kingdom. Holy One, I realize You never promised that I would live a life free of sorrow. In fact, You tell me in Your Word, "In this life you will have sorrow." When I walk through the fire, remind me that You are with me. I know that Your primary purpose in my life is transformation into the image of Your Son, Jesus. I bow before You, Lord, and ask You to use the suffering to shape my heart more fully to beat to the rhythm of Jesus'.

*(Psalm 66:10–12; John 16:33; Romans 8:29)*

*You are the God
who performs miracles;
you display your power
among the peoples.*

PSALM 77:14

At different points in our lives, the situation looks hopeless. This was true for my friend Bonnie.

Bonnie had a stroke while waterskiing, and though hundreds were praying, the situation looked dire. The morning after Bonnie had her stroke, I woke early in the morning to pray for her. Honestly, my heart was in the pit of doubt and darkness. I stayed on my knees for a long time weeping and begging God to heal my friend. After a few hours, I sensed the Holy Spirit prompt my heart:

"Becky, I want you to shift your prayers to praise. Praise Me for the healing I am doing in Bonnie's life."

Huh? I wasn't sure I understood correctly. But I turned on the song "I Raise a Hallelujah" and began—by faith—praising God with all my might. What happened was nothing short of miraculous! Despite the doctor's prognosis that she wouldn't survive the night after her stroke, Bonnie began showing signs of responsiveness that next morning. In the following days and weeks, she would gradually begin the long journey toward recovery. Her physical therapists have said to her, "Your recovery is amazing and remarkable given the severity of the stroke." Bonnie's story is being used by God in mighty ways that I can't even describe. Through her long journey, Bonnie and her husband, Jim, have praised God. Their new normal is a testimony to many of the faithfulness of God.

Now, I want to be clear. God doesn't always heal this side of heaven. And praise should not be manipulative in nature to get our way. Praise brings our hearts into a place of trusting the Lord for whatever outcome He brings. He calls us to praise Him by faith in advance of Him working. Having said that, God is still the God of miracles. Nothing is impossible for Him. When we choose to praise

Him by faith, He stirs up deeper faith in our hearts.

The psalmist wrote, "You are the God who performs miracles" (Ps. 77:14). In another psalm we read, "Who formed the mountains by your power, having armed yourself with strength, who stilled the roaring of the seas, the roaring of their waves, and the turmoil of the nations" (Ps. 65:6–7). When the situation feels hopeless, remember that God is the almighty God who lacks nothing. Praise Him by faith. His plan might not look like what you're expecting, but His character remains the same. He is *still* almighty God, with whom nothing is impossible. Bow before Him and worship!

**Selah—Pause and Reflect:** *What impossible situation are you facing in your life right now? What does it look like for you to trust the God of miracles?*

**Today's Truth:** *Praise God that nothing is impossible for God. Ask Him to stir up renewed faith in your spirit.*

**Listen:** *"Raise a Hallelujah" sung by Jonathan David Helser and Melissa Helser, Bethel Music*

**Pray:** Lord God, I praise You that nothing, absolutely nothing, is impossible for You. You are the one who crafted the majestic mountains, shaped the planets, and flung the stars into space. You still the stormy sea with just a word and calm the nations with the snap of Your finger. You are almighty God and the Bread of Life. You calm me with Your whisper and deliver me from evil. You're faithful in Your love and good in all Your ways. You are infinite in Your wisdom and just in all Your actions. No one compares with You and no one competes with You. Only You are the God of miracles. You alone are worthy of all my praise. Nothing is too difficult for You.

*(Genesis 1:1; Psalm 65:6–7; Jeremiah 32:17; John 6:35)*

*They remembered that God*
*was their Rock,*
*that God Most High*
*was their Redeemer.*

PSALM 78:35

Every now and then I get a notification from Facebook inviting me to look back to an event a few years prior. It says, "Rediscover this day!" Ah, that's a great discipline for our spiritual journeys. When you're in the wilderness and circumstances look dark, that is the time to look back and practice the worship of remembrance.

The psalmist reminds us that when the people of God were wandering in the wilderness, God provided for them. He divided the sea so they could pass through on dry ground (Ps. 78:13). He led them with the cloud of His holy presence by day, sheltering them from the heat of the desert, and with the fire of His presence by night, providing heat to warm them in the cold desert winds (Ps. 78:14). He split the rock in two and provided abundant water for their thirst (Ps. 78:15–16). He rained down manna from heaven to satisfy their hunger (Ps. 78:23–24). He brought birds from the east and west to fill their craving for meat (Ps. 78:26–29). Then the psalmist says, "In spite of all this, they kept on sinning" (Ps. 78:32). But then, "They remembered" (Ps. 78:35).

Friend, when life is the darkest, it's time to remember! In the worship of remembrance, we look back, and we intentionally bring to mind how God has been faithful in the past. He has a proven track record. Use your mind to govern your emotions. Ask yourself, "Has God provided in the past?" If He has, would He suddenly change His character now? Certainly not. He will be faithful today and tomorrow as well.

The worship of remembrance reminds us that we can trust the God who is faithful.

**Selah—Pause and Reflect:** *Spend a few minutes reflecting on how God has provided for you. Make a list, and keep it in your Bible to remind yourself often that He has been faithful in the past, and He will be faithful today.*

**Today's Truth:** *Praise God for His faithfulness. Practice the worship of remembrance.*

**Listen:** *"Goodness of God" sung by Jenn Johnson, Bethel Music*

**Pray:** Father God, I praise You for Your constant faithfulness in my life. I remember when _____

_____

_____ [write in the blank the times when God has been faithful in providing for you]. I worship You, Lord Jesus. You are always faithful and constantly good. I praise You that even when I fail, You are faithful to forgive. I thank You for the times when I've been down to the wire and the situation felt dire, but You provided. I praise You that Your very nature is faithfulness. I praise You that You faithfully protect me from the evil one and that all You call me to, You faithfully provide for.

*(1 Corinthians 1:9; 1 John 1:9; 1 Thessalonians 5:24; 2 Thessalonians 3:3)*

*I will listen
to what God the LORD says;
he promises peace to his people,
his faithful servants—
but let them not turn to folly.*

PSALM 85:8

Listening is challenging for many of us. We have so many thoughts and ideas in our head that we just love to talk. Right? But unless we bow before the Prince of Peace, we cannot hear and experience the peace He promises.

God's voice comes to us in a variety of ways. Certainly He speaks through the Scriptures. At times, He speaks through a friend and we may know instantly, "God is speaking to me through this person." Or He might speak to us through a great sermon or worship song. Our spirit resonates with the Holy Spirit, and we know God is speaking. Sometimes He gets our attention through unmet expectations. This was true for King David.

David's desire was to build a grand and glorious temple (2 Sam. 7:1–5). He shared his desire with the prophet Nathan. While Nathan thought it a great idea at first, after a few days, he came back to David and told him the Lord had a different plan. Instead of David building the temple, David's son Solomon would. What was David's response to this disappointing news? Scripture tells us, "Then King David went in and sat before the LORD" (2 Sam. 7:18). He bowed his will as an act of worship.

Only as we bow our expectations before the Lord in worship will we experience the peace the Lord promises.

**Selah—Pause and Reflect:** *When your expectations of God are not met, how do you respond? Do you sit in His presence to listen, or do you pull back from His presence?*

**Today's Truth:** *When God doesn't live up to your expectations, instead of pulling back, sit in His presence and worship Him.*

**Listen:** *"At Your Whisper" sung by Meredith Andrews, The Belonging Co*

**Pray:** Holy, almighty God, I confess that sometimes I don't understand Your ways. I have, whether consciously or unconsciously, placed expectations on You. But You are vastly "other." Your wisdom, no one can fathom. Who has known Your mind? Or who has ever been Your counselor? You have said that Your ways are not my ways. You alone know what's best for me, my family, our nation, and our world. I bow before You, King of kings and Lord of lords. When I feel disappointed, help me to sit before You and to bow my will in favor of Yours. There I will find the peace You have promised.

*(Psalm 85:8; Isaiah 55:8; Romans 11:34–36)*

*Blessed are those*
*whose strength is in you,*
*whose hearts are set on pilgrimage.*
*As they pass through the*
*Valley of Baka,*
*they make it a place of springs; the*
*autumn rains also cover it with pools.*
*They go from strength to strength . . .*

PSALM 84:5–7a

A pilgrimage is a spiritual journey. The psalmist writes of pilgrimage as a journey to experience the deeper presence of God. Here's the thing about a pilgrimage: you have to intentionally set your heart on continuing because the pilgrimage will have wonderful moments as well as dreadful moments. If, however, you persevere even when the journey feels difficult, you will be blessed with a strength that can only come from God.

The psalmist writes about a person who has set their heart to pursue God's presence. Their journey leads them through the Valley of Baka. Baka is a type of balsam plant that can survive in very dry conditions. The Valley of Baka refers to a deserted place or a place of intense hardship. It is a valley of weeping. Ever been there? I sure have. I remember a season in my life when I felt like all I did was cry. The journey felt so arduous and difficult. Each morning on my knees, my worship was my weeping.

The hope is that as we persist in worship, even in the valley of weeping, it ultimately becomes a place of blessing. There on your face before God, the Holy Spirit exchanges your losses for His blessings. The brightness of Christ's glorious presence shines through even the darkest hour (Ps. 18:12). You come to the startling realization that He is enough. You are strengthened in your journey, and you emerge a more resolute and resilient pilgrim.

**Selah—Pause and Reflect:** *What does it look like for you to resolutely set your heart on a pilgrimage to pursue God's presence?*

**Today's Truth:** *As you praise and worship the Lord even in the valley of weeping, it becomes a place of blessing.*

**Listen:** *"Worthy of It All" sung by Jeremy Riddle*

**Pray:** Lord Jesus, I long to experience more of Your glorious presence. My soul yearns for more of You. I know that means I need to passionately pursue You above all else. In seasons of chaos, I realize I go into "survival" mode, pursuing solutions instead of pursuing You as Savior. Lord, the place where You dwell is lovely. In Your presence, there is peace and hope even in the darkest trial. When I'm tempted to quit the pilgrimage to experience Your presence more deeply, help me to remember that the valley of weeping ultimately becomes a place of blessing. True happiness is found in You!

*(Psalm 63:1; 84:1, 5–6)*

*But you,* LORD, *are a compassionate
and gracious God,
slow to anger, abounding
in love and faithfulness.* . . .
*Give me a sign of your goodness.*

PSALM 86:15, 17

Lost. I was lost, and I desperately needed a sign telling me where to go. I had to get to the event on time. I whispered a rather panicked prayer, "Lord, please help! Show me the exit to turn on so I arrive on time." Ever prayed a prayer like that? Yup. I'm guessing you have.

It's one thing to pray for a sign when we're lost driving and GPS is sending us around and around in circles, but what about when life sends us around and around in circles? With our faith quaking, doubt pounces. We feel desperate for a sign of God's goodness. But is it right to pray for a sign?

I heard many sermons when I was young about how you need to just have faith and not ask God for a sign. I heard the story of Gideon who put out a fleece before the Lord (Judg. 6:33–40). The preachers I heard all seemed to condemn him for his lack of faith. Here's the thing: all of us have weak moments when our faith shakes.

Rather than condemning ourselves for those moments—when we cry out in agony, "Lord, give me a sign of Your goodness!"—I believe we ought to receive God's grace and compassionate love instead. He who created us is mindful that we are dust (Ps. 103:14). I fear sometimes that we put unrealistic expectations on ourselves, and in so doing we are tempted to deny what we're really feeling. Denying our feelings and the authentic cries of our hearts is religiosity, not a genuine relationship with God.

God invites us to bring our authentic selves into His presence: the good, the bad, the ugly. There, as we lament and plead for a sign of His goodness, He compassionately loves us and comforts us.

Friend, beating yourself up for not having strong enough faith is worse in my opinion than simply asking God to remind you of His goodness and faithfulness. He knows you are human, and sometimes your faith is weak. Turn toward Him in those moments, and dare to be honest.

**Selah—Pause and Reflect:** *Do you beat yourself up when doubt comes your way? How does that help you?*

**Today's Truth:** *God is so gracious and compassionate. When we cry out for a sign of His goodness, He understands.*

**Listen:** *"Peace Be Still" sung by Hope Darst*

**Pray:** Loving Lord Jesus, I praise You that You are compassionate. Thank You for grace when my doubts defeat me. I praise You that Your love is as high as the heavens and that You remove our sins as far as the east is from the west. I praise You that those who look to You are radiant and their faces are never covered with shame. Lord, thank You that I don't have to give way to shame. When I sink into doubt and beg You for a sign of Your goodness, You understand. As I look with eyes of faith for a sign or word from You, You are delighted with my faith. You understand how frail my human faith is, and You say that even faith the size of a mustard seed is great. I will praise You as long as I live.

*(Psalm 34:5; 86:15; 103:11)*

*Satisfy us in the morning*
*with your unfailing love,*
*that we may sing for joy and be glad*
*all our days.*

PSALM 90:14

There is so much to know of God's love that, even in the moments when we feel completely loved, there's more. A. W. Tozer wrote of the knowledge of the love of God stretching out before us like a vast ocean. No matter how deep we dive, we can go deeper still.

Moses wrote Psalm 90 during the time he was leading the children of Israel through the desert to the Promised Land. The challenges of leadership, as well as the difficulty of navigating the barren desert, led Moses to express the deep longing to be more satisfied with God's love: "Satisfy us in the morning with your unfailing love" (Ps. 90:14).

I remember a season in my life when I knew intellectually that God loved me. After all, the Bible told me He did, which meant He was under contractual agreement to love me. But I wrestled with this: Could a God so vast *feel* love for me emotionally? Was it a cold, distant, non-emotional sort of love that merely put up with me?

As I studied God's Word, praised God by faith for His love, and continually cried out for more of His love, I began to realize that God's love was deeply emotional. He longed for me with an ache in His heart. He felt for me beyond what the most romantic lover would feel. And His desire was for me to not only know His love intellectually, but also to *feel* and experience His love for me. This was the apostle Paul's desire for the Ephesian believers, that their roots would go down deep into God's love and they would have the power to understand and experience how wide and long and deep God's love was for them (Eph. 3:17–19).

Friend, God's desire for you is that you *feel* so satisfied with His love that you would go through life singing.

**Selah—Pause and Reflect:** *Is it easy or difficult for you to feel God's love for you?*

**Today's Truth:** *God wants me to not just know in my head that He loves me. He wants me to feel His love in my heart.*

**Listen:** *"Reckless Love" sung by Cory Asbury*

**Pray:** Lord Jesus, I praise You that You love me. I feel as if I've only tasted Your love, but I long to experience more. I confess, Lord, that often, though I know in my head that You love me, I can't seem to feel it in my heart. I know that my feelings don't determine the truth of Your loving me, but I long, with Moses, to experience Your love more. Satisfy my longings, I pray. Let me experience with all believers how high and wide and deep and long Your love is for me. Holy One, may I feel Your unfailing, never-ending love surrounding and enveloping me as I go through my day.

*(Psalm 33:22; 34:8; 90:14; Ephesians 3:18)*

*It is good to praise the LORD*
*and make music to your name,*
*O Most High,*
*proclaiming your love in the morning*
*and your faithfulness at night.*

PSALM 92:1–2

One of the best ways to crush anxiety is to develop regular rhythms of praise. When we praise God, fear is quieted and courage gains a voice. The early church practiced regular rhythms of turning to God through prayer and praise. The church fathers called this "the daily office" and believed it was the first priority of believers to be with God.

The psalmist also suggests regular rhythms of praise, encouraging us to develop the habit of proclaiming God's love in the morning and His faithfulness at night (Ps. 92:2). This is a rather easy way to enfold each day in praise to the Lord. When you first wake up, praise God for His love, and as you lay your head down to sleep at night, praise Him for His faithfulness.

The rhythm of morning and evening praise will help to protect your heart in the day of difficulty. When fear and anxiety come knocking, fixed moments of praise will help settle your heart and keep your focus on the Lord.

The prophet Daniel was a captive of King Nebuchadnezzar of Babylon. As a prisoner of a pagan ruler, it would have been easy to wrestle with anxiety and fear. Certainly, when Daniel refused to direct his prayers to the king and he was thrown into the lion's den, it would be normal to feel terrified. What kept Daniel steady and strong? I believe it was his regular rhythms of prayer and praise. Three times a day, Daniel got on his knees to pray and give thanks to the Lord (Dan. 6:10). Our regular rhythms of praise keep us steady when the days are uncertain.

You don't have to start with three times a day. Begin

with the rhythm of two times a day: morning and evening. In the morning, as you enter the new day, focus your attention on Christ and celebrate His love for you. In the evening, as you lay down to sleep, praise Him for His faithfulness. As you develop a regular rhythm of morning and evening praise, you will find it's not stressful. It's delightful, brings great joy, and honors God.

**Selah—Pause and Reflect:** *As you think about your life, how might intentionally practicing morning and evening rhythms of praise enhance your peace and awareness of the presence of God?*

**Today's Truth:** *Developing an intentional rhythm of morning and evening praise will deepen your peace and your awareness of God's presence.*

**Listen:** *"From Whom All Blessings Flow (Doxology)" sung by Hillsong Worship*

**Pray:** Oh, Lord God, I'm hungry for more of You. I want to know You more completely and experience Your presence more fully. Lord, help me as I intentionally develop rhythms of praise. Let me listen for Your voice of love first thing in the morning and keep the joy of it in my heart all day long. Remind me day by day to worship You for Your love every morning and to praise You in the evening for Your faithfulness. Your lovingkindness endures all day long. I want to be like the psalmist who said, "In the morning I will sing of your love." Oh, Lord, let my life be a song of praise to You. I praise You that, through every day and every circumstance, You are good. Every sunrise speaks of Your love, and every sunset speaks of Your faithfulness. I kneel before You in worship.

*(Psalm 59:16; 63:1; 92:1; 95:6; 143:8)*

*The LORD reigns, let the earth be glad;*
*let the distant shores rejoice.*
*Clouds and thick*
*darkness surround him;*
*righteousness and justice*
*are the foundation of his throne.*

PSALM 97:1–2

When life feels uncertain or chaotic, I need the reminder that the Lord reigns. What about you? Sometimes it just feels like life spins out of control and everything goes wonky. Right?! In those moments, we can feel as though we're free falling. But the truth is, God is not caught off guard, nor is He ever surprised. He is sovereignly in control. He doesn't take a day off, nor does He get distracted.

The psalmist reminds us that the Lord reigns. Pause for just a second and consider that. He reigns. No matter who is in political power, no matter what happens in the economy, no matter what disease breaks out or natural disasters occur, *God reigns.* And He is a completely righteous and just ruler!

The apostle Paul put it this way: "God, who is the blessed controller of all things, the king over all kings and the master of all masters, the only source of immortality, the one who lives in unapproachable light. . . . To him be acknowledged all honour and power for ever, amen!" (1 Tim. 6:15–16 Phillips).

Friend, the circumstances in your life might feel horrific right now. You might be facing unimaginable difficulties and utter darkness. God is still in control. Nothing catches Him off guard. He is the one "who lives in unapproachable light" (1 Tim. 6:16). He promises to guard the lives of those who love Him (Ps. 97:10). He promises to turn every painful circumstance around for our good (Rom. 8:28). Rest in His promises today!

**Selah—Pause and Reflect:** *When life spins out of control, what is your normal, go-to coping mechanism? What would it look like for you to praise God that He reigns, even in the midst of uncertainty?*

**Today's Truth:** *God reigns. You can trust Him when life spins out of control.*

**Listen:** *"What You Said" sung by Jon Egan*

**Pray:** Lord God, I confess, when life spins out of control, I feel afraid. Holy One, I praise You that You reign, and nothing catches You by surprise. I exalt You for being the blessed controller of all things! Thank You that righteousness and justice are the foundation of Your throne. I know that everything You do is good, and You will turn around even the painful circumstances in my life and use them for my good. I rest in Your promises today. Thank You that You promise to guard the lives of those who love You. Guard my heart from fear and anxiety today. Fill me with joy and gladness as I praise You today!

*(Psalm 97:1, 10, 12; Romans 8:28; 1 Timothy 6:15)*

*I will sing of your love and justice;*
*to you, LORD, I will sing praise. . . .*
*Every morning*
*I will put to silence*
*all the wicked in the land.*

PSALM 101:1, 8

The place where Satan most torments believers is in our minds. He messes with our thinking, sending thoughts of anxiety, fear, self-doubt, and God-doubt. However, God has given us the incredible power of choice. In other words, we have a choice about what thoughts our mind will entertain.

The psalmist writes, "I will sing of your love and justice" (Ps. 101:1). Notice the word "will." In fact, why don't you circle it in the verses? The word "will" implies a choice. When life is tough, we don't always feel like shouting an exuberant "Hallelujah! God is good!" We don't always feel like praising God or singing.

That is when our power of choice has to govern our feelings. I may not feel like being exuberant, but I can choose to pray, "God, I praise You that You are good though my circumstances don't feel good." When life feels dark, we can choose to put on worship music in our homes and allow the music to prompt our praise. In other words, we do not have to give in to the thoughts Satan may be throwing at us. We can intentionally choose to direct our thoughts to the lovingkindness and graciousness of God. This is the way we, in the words of the psalmist, "put to silence all the wicked" (Ps. 101:8). We choose to take every thought captive (2 Cor. 10:5). When we direct our thoughts to God, choosing to praise Him for His goodness though life may feel bad, we find peace in His presence.

**Selah—Pause and Reflect:** *How does Satan most often attack your thinking? What will be your method of combat in the future?*

**Today's Truth:** *Praise is a choice. We can choose to praise God and keep our thoughts captive to truth by an act of our will, even when life feels uncertain.*

**Listen:** *"I Exalt Thee" sung by Jesus Image Worship | Jesus '19*

**Pray:** Holy One, I praise You for designing my mind with the ability to make choices. Oh, Father, You are so good to me! Thank You that I can choose where my thoughts will be centered. I praise You that as I fix my focus on Jesus, the author and finisher of my faith, that You will quiet anxiety and fear. Thank You that as I praise You, Satan will run. Oh, Lord, I thank You that I am protected by Your blood and that no weapon formed against me will prosper. I praise You that as I take every thought captive and focus my mind on praising You, my heart will follow. I praise You for the gift of Your Holy Spirit who strengthens my faith and gives me hope as I praise You.

*(Deuteronomy 30:19; Isaiah 54:17; Romans 5:5; 2 Corinthians 10:5; Hebrews 12:2)*

*Praise the LORD, my soul,*
*and forget not all his benefits—*
*who forgives all your sins*
*and heals all your diseases,*
*who redeems your life from the pit*
*and crowns you with*
*love and compassion,*
*who satisfies your*
*desires with good things*
*so that your youth is*
*renewed like the eagle's.*

PSALM 103:2–5

Praise increases our faith and also prepares our hearts for God to work on our behalf. In some ways, it is actually addictive . . . and it's meant to be. As we faithfully praise God, a beautiful cycle of worship develops in our lives. A great example of this cycle is found in Psalm 103.

David reflects on and praises God for all the wonderful ways He has worked in David's life. The more David praises, the more the Holy Spirit unleashes feelings of gratitude in David. And as those feelings of gratitude well up in him, he praises God even more. What David models for us in Psalm 103 is the cycle of ceaseless praise.

Anxiety can also be cyclical in our lives. You begin to worry. From the one worry, you begin to consider all the "what ifs". Before you know it, you're in a full-blown panic attack. If you continue to focus on the potential scenarios, this practice will form the pattern of your thinking. You need to break the cycle by redirecting your thoughts. Your thoughts need to be re-focused on Jesus. This will take intentionality. The moment worry enters, turn it over to God and start praising Him.

Echo David's words, "Praise the LORD, my soul" (Ps. 103:1). Think of all the ways God has blessed you: He's forgiven your sins. He's loved you eternally. He's provided for your needs. He's able to heal your diseases. His love never ends. He's never left you nor abandoned you (Heb. 13:5).

As you launch your thinking into the cycle of praise, you will actually feel the difference. You'll notice a shift happening in your brain. Fear will turn to courage, doubt to faith, and anxiety to calm. You will find your heart more aligned with God's, and your desires will be satisfied because they will be God's desires for you.

The best part is that as you praise Him, it will awaken a greater desire in your soul for more of Him. Gradually, as you continue, a new habit will form. Rather than being addicted to worry, you'll be "addicted" to praising God. And that, my friend, is a win!

**Selah—Pause and Reflect:** *How does the cycle of anxiety get the best of you? How can you stop the cycle of worry and adopt the cycle of praise instead?*

**Today's Truth:** *You have the ability to stop the cycle of fear and anxiety by putting into practice the cycle of praise.*

**Listen:** *"Seated on High" sung by Andrew Holt and The Belonging Co*

**Pray:** I worship and praise You, Lord God! You are good, gracious, and holy. You have blessed my life in so many ways _____

_____

_____

_ [list some ways God has blessed your life in the past few years]. I praise You for how You forgive all my sins and continually have compassion on me as a loving Father. I thank You for all the gifts You have given me—gifts of both provision and empowerment. I praise You that, from everlasting to everlasting, Your love and faithfulness remain the same. I praise You that in heaven all the angelic beings bow before Your throne and sing a continual chorus of "Holy, Holy, Holy." Oh, Lord, You are worthy of all my praise. When I start to worry today, empower me to capture those worries, hand them over to You, and then bow down and worship You. As I create a new cycle of thought patterns, may my meditation be pleasing to You. Lord, I thank You that as I praise You, panic will diminish in Jesus' name!

*(Psalm 103:1, 5, 11, 13, 17; 104:34; Revelation 4:8)*

*The LORD made his people
very fruitful.*

PSALM 105:24

As I write this, we are on day forty-one of the COVID-19 quarantine. Shelter-in-place orders have kept us largely cooped up in our homes. During this season in what feels like "house arrest," many have been asking, "How do I stay productive and fruitful during this season?" As I've considered this, my mind traveled back to the children of Israel when they were in captivity in Egypt. There, under the cruel rule of Pharaoh and in dire circumstances, the Lord made His people very fruitful!

The prophet Habakkuk experienced similar circumstances, yet He made this declaration: "Though the fig tree does not bud and there are no grapes on the vines, though the olive crop fails and the fields produce no food, though there are no sheep in the pen and no cattle in the stalls, yet I will rejoice in the LORD, I will be joyful in God my Savior. The Sovereign LORD is my strength; he makes my feet like the feet of a deer, he enables me to tread on the heights" (Hab. 3:17–19).

Habakkuk made a choice to praise God and rejoice in the Lord. As a result, the inner fruit of faith was developed in his life. It wasn't financially profitable fruit; it was the fruit of deep trust in God and resiliency that was woven into Habakkuk's life. This fruitfulness allowed him to stand strong and confident while facing the impending doom of the Babylonians coming against Judah.

In your life and mine, there will be seasons of difficulty and discouragement. Our circumstances may be dark, and we may feel like we're in captivity to anxiety. It may seem as though all of life has turned against us and the situation is dire. At times like this, the posture of worship is open hands and a surrendered heart. Out of that posture, the Holy Spirit can bring the fruitfulness of resiliency, which will allow us to soar with strong faith.

**Selah—Pause and Reflect:** *Read Habakkuk's declaration slowly. Then rewrite it as it applies to your specific situation. For example, "Though there are no job openings on the horizon and no reserves in the bank . . ."*

**Today's Truth:** *Even in times of great difficulty and pain, God can make us fruitful if we choose to praise Him.*

**Listen:** *"New Wine" sung by Hillsong Worship*

**Pray:** Father God, I recognize that every good and perfect gift comes from You. I realize I must receive these gifts with open hands and a surrendered heart. You are the one who gives, and You are the one who takes away. I praise You that even when I have been stripped of many of the comforts of life, I can consider all of it loss compared to the joy of knowing You. I praise You that even when circumstances are uncertain, You are able to produce fruitfulness in my life. I need only to keep my focus on abiding in You. You have promised that as I keep my heart fixed on You, You will produce fruit in my life. Apart from You, no fruit is worthwhile. Just as You made the children of Israel very fruitful while they were living in captivity, You are able to do the same for me. Holy Spirit, I praise You for the fruit of resiliency that You are growing in my life.

*(Psalm 105:24; John 15:4–5; Philippians 3:7–10; James 1:17)*

*Search me, God, and know my heart;*
*test me and know my anxious thoughts.*
*See if there is any offensive way in me,*
*and lead me in the way everlasting.*

PSALM 139:23–24

I love this prayer of David's and have often started my morning worship time with his words, "Search me, God, and know my heart; test me and know my anxious thoughts." And then added my own: "See if there is any area of hidden anxiety that needs to be healed by You."

Hidden anxieties can create traps for us. They can be healed by the Holy Healer, but only as we ask God to reveal the truth about where they are lurking. Often those places of hidden anxieties are attached to vows we've made to not experience pain again. Such vows are unhealthy. They need to be demolished because they become strongholds in our lives that are contrary to the knowledge of God (2 Cor. 10:5).

What are some of the unhealthy vows we make when we're afraid? We might vow to never be hurt again so we construct a wall around our heart. As a result, we fail to love like Jesus. We may vow to never suffer financial loss again, so we focus on building a large nest egg and let go of generosity. We may vow to never take a risk again, even though to follow Jesus is a risk and requires faith. There are hundreds of unhealthy vows that we make when we feel anxious.

The only way to free ourselves from the strangling hold of these vows is to ask the Lord to search us and bring them to light. As He reveals the truth about any hidden anxieties and we renounce the unhealthy vows we've made, we acknowledge Christ as Lord of our heart through praise.

**Selah—Pause and Reflect:** *Consider what unhealthy vows you've made that were birthed out of anxiety or fear. What does it look like for you to renounce those vows?*

**Today's Truth:** *Dare to ask the Holy Spirit to search you and reveal any hidden pockets of anxiety and the unhealthy vows you've made attached to those fears.*

**Listen:** *"Holy Spirit" sung by Kari Jobe and Cody Carnes*

**Pray:** Holy Spirit, search my heart. I lay my heart and mind before You as an open book. Search my mind and heart, and reveal to me any places where hidden anxiety lurks. Show me the unhealthy vows I've made in response to those fears. Lord, I don't want to keep any vow that stands contrary to Your lordship in my life. I want to demolish every false argument and pretense that I have set up in my thinking to protect me. I renounce now every unhealthy vow _____

_____ [write

in the vows you have made]. I acknowledge that You truly are Lord of my life. When I feel tempted toward self-protection or preservation, help me to remember that You hold my life in Your hands. I bow to Your will for my life in every area. When anxiety threatens my thinking, I will fix my eyes on Your character and put my trust in You. I worship and give You thanks, my Lord of lords.

*(Psalm 56:3; 136:3; 139:23–24; 2 Corinthians 10:5)*

*I will exalt you, my God the King;*
*I will praise your name*
*for ever and ever.*
*Every day I will praise you*
*and extol your name*
*for ever and ever.*
*Great is the LORD*
*and most worthy of praise;*
*his greatness no one can fathom.*
*One generation commends*
*your works to another;*
*they tell of your mighty acts.*

PSALM 145:1–4

Every great relationship takes commitment, and it's the same in your relationship with God. The psalmist writes exuberantly that he will choose to exalt God and praise His name every day. God is so great and so matchless in His worth that He is worthy of all your praise.

As you consistently turn your panic into praise, you will change. Anxiety will melt in His presence and fear will dissipate. You will become the calm, steady person described in Jeremiah 17:7–8: "Blessed is the one who trusts in the LORD, whose confidence is in him. They will be like a tree planted by the water that sends out its roots by the stream. It does not fear when heat comes; its leaves are always green. It has no worries in a year of drought and never fails to bear fruit."

Friend, only He can establish that kind of calm in your life. As you faithfully worship Him, you will become more like Him.

He is the Alpha and the Omega and your Bread of Life.

He's your Creator and Deliverer who is eternally loving and faithful.

He is completely good and categorically holy.

He is infinitely wise and just in all His ways.

He is the King of kings and the Lord of lords.

He is mighty enough to save you and tender enough to hear the faintest whisper of your heart.

He is opulent in His splendor and powerful in His glory.

He quiets you with His love and declares you righteous with His blood.

He saves you from your sin and shepherds you when you wander.

He is absolute Truth while being completely understanding.

He is Victory over sin, hell, and the grave.

He is the Wonderful Counselor and almighty God.

He is the Matchless Exalted One who yields His glory to no other.

He is the One with the name that is above every name.

And He is the only One worthy of all your praise!

**Selah—Pause and Reflect:** *How might continuing consistent patterns of praise contribute to your becoming calm?*

**Today's Truth:** *He is worthy of all our praise. As you worship Him, you will become calm and steady in spite of life's storms.*

**Listen:** *"Is He Worthy?" sung by Andrew Peterson and "The Blessing" sung by Kari Jobe and Cody Carnes, Elevation Worship*

**Pray:** I exalt You, my God, the King! Lord, my heart echoes the cry of angels in heaven, "Holy, Holy, Holy is the Lord God Almighty, who was and is and is to come . . . You are worthy!" (Rev. 4:8, 11). You alone created all things and sustain all things. You are the only One worthy to open the scroll because by Your blood, You purchased people from every nation, tribe, and tongue. You have made us a kingdom of priests to serve others. Honor and glory and blessing belong to You, Lord Jesus. You have purchased me and made me righteous with Your blood. I am complete in You. I am hidden in You and seated with You at the right hand of God. I praise You, Lord Jesus, because You grant me victory over anxiety as I nurture my body, soul, and spirit. Thank You that You give me tools such as praise, exercise, and even medicine or natural supplements to aid me in my journey. You have all authority over any anxiety that threatens to unravel me. Great and marvelous are Your deeds, Lord God Almighty. May I continue to live my life as a praise song to You! You alone are worthy of all my praise!

*(Psalm 145:1; Colossians 3:3; Revelation 4:8, 11; 5:9–10; 15:3)*

# LIST OF PRAISE SONGS

Listening to praise music helps turn our minds and hearts to worship our God and prompts our praise. In each day's devotional, I've suggested a song to listen to. Below is a handy list of all those songs and suggestions for worship bands or recording artists in case you'd like to create a playlist on your favorite music platform.

Day 1     "I Will Praise You" sung by Hillsong Worship and "Take Courage" sung by Kristene DiMarco

Day 2     "With You" sung by Elevation Worship

Day 3     "Just Want You" sung by Sarah Reeves and The Belonging Co

Day 4     "Isn't He" sung by Natalie Grant and The Belonging Co

Day 5     "I Know" sung by Big Daddy Weave

Day 6     "Be Strong" sung by Jon Egan

Day 7     "Hiding Place" sung by All Peoples
          Worship, featuring Keri Denison

Day 8     "You Say" sung by Lauren Daigle

Day 9     "In Christ Alone" sung by Geoff Moore and
          The Distance

Day 10    "Take Over" sung by Shane & Shane

Day 11    "Oh Praise the Name" sung by Hillsong
          Worship

Day 12    "What a Beautiful Name" sung by Brooke
          Fraser Ligertwood and Hillsong Worship

Day 13    "Surrounded" sung by Kari Jobe and
          "Psalm 46 (Lord of Hosts)" sung by Shane
          & Shane

Day 14    "No One Beside/Have My Heart" sung by
          Elevation Worship

Day 15    "Available" sung by Elevation Worship and
          "Promises" sung by Maverick City/Tribal

Day 16    "There Is a King" sung by Elevation Worship

Day 17    "Christ Be Magnified" sung by Cody Carnes

Day 18    "Raise a Hallelujah" sung by Jonathan David
          Helser & Melissa Helser, Bethel Music

Day 19   "Goodness of God" sung by Jenn Johnson, Bethel Music

Day 20   "At Your Whisper" sung by Meredith Andrews, The Belonging Co

Day 21   "Worthy of It All" sung by Jeremy Riddle

Day 22   "Peace Be Still" sung by Hope Darst

Day 23   "Reckless Love" sung by Cory Asbury

Day 24   "From Whom All Blessings Flow (Doxology)" sung by Hillsong Worship

Day 25   "What You Said" sung by Jon Egan

Day 26   "I Exalt Thee" sung by Jesus Image Worship | Jesus '19

Day 27   "Seated on High" sung by Andrew Holt and The Belonging Co

Day 28   "New Wine" sung by Hillsong Worship

Day 29   "Holy Spirit" sung by Kari Jobe and Cody Carnes

Day 30   "Is He Worthy?" sung by Andrew Peterson and "The Blessing" sung by Kari Jobe and Cody Carnes, Elevation Worship

# ACKNOWLEDGMENTS

Special thanks to my husband, Steve. Thanks for cheering me on as I write and for loving me so well. I love you!

Our kids: Bethany and Chris, Josiah and Shaina, Stefanie and Dave, Keri and Zach—all of you are amazing, and I love how you faithfully praise God through every uncertain moment in your lives.

Our grandkids: Charlie, Tyler, Joshua, Selah, Zachary, Theo, Noah, Rayna, Cayden, Kinley, Tori, Melody, Asher and Austin—I love you all more than words can express! May each of you grow up to love Jesus and praise Him faithfully.

Bonnie Gordon: Thanks for allowing me to use your story. You are such an example of praising God through uncertain times! Love you, friend.

Blythe Daniel: Not only are you my agent, but you are my dear friend who faithfully prays! Love you!

Judy Dunagan: In addition to being the acquisition editor for this, you are my precious friend. Our friendship is a treasure to me! Love you!

Amanda Cleary: You're such a joy to work with in the editing process. I'm so grateful for you!

All the men and women at Moody Publishers who made this book possible. I love working with you!

# NOTES

1. Dallas Willard, *Life Without Lack* (Nashville: Nelson Books, 2018), 97.

2. Strong's Concordance #571, https://biblehub.com/hebrew/571.htm.

3. Peter Scazzero, *Emotionally Healthy Relationships Day by Day* (Grand Rapids: Zondervan, 2017), 119.

4. Corrie ten Boom, Elizabeth and John Sherrill, *The Hiding Place* (Bloomington, MN: Chosen Books, 1974), 190.

5. Ruth Myers, *31 Days of Drawing Near to God: Resting Securely in His Delight* (Colorado Springs: Multnomah, 1999), 81.

# Do you know Jesus as He really is?

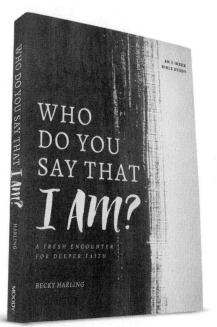

# GET THE RESOURCES YOU NEED FOR WHEN LIFE TAKES AN UNEXPECTED TURN.

**5 SIMPLE WAYS TO STRENGTHEN YOUR MARRIAGE**
... When You're Stuck at Home Together
A LOVE LANGUAGE RESOURCE
Gary Chapman
#1 New York Times bestselling author of The Love Languages

978-0-8024-2332-0

**PSALMS FOR THE ANXIOUS HEART**
A 30-Day Devotional for Uncertain Times
Becky Harling

978-0-8024-2338-2

**WHAT NOW?**
How to Move into Your Next Season
Mark Jobe

978-0-8024-2341-2

**THE CHURCH RECOVERY GUIDE**
How Your Congregation Can Adapt and Thrive after a Crisis
Karl Vaters

978-0-8024-2343-6

**open** THE BIBLE in 30 days
Colin S. Smith

978-0-8024-2344-3

**PANDEMICS, PLAGUES, AND NATURAL DISASTERS**
What is GOD Saying to Us?
Erwin W. Lutzer

978-0-8024-2345-0

**HOW TO PRAY IN A CRISIS**
A 4-Step Guide to Renewal
Daniel Henderson
FOREWORD BY MARK VROEGOP

978-0-8024-2359-7

**WITHOUT A DOUBT**
How to Know for Certain That You're Good with God
Dean Inserra

978-0-8024-2360-3

Be it in the midst of a natural disaster, global unrest, or an unforeseen pandemic, the repercussions of unprecedented change can leave us all reeling. Get the wisdom, encouragement, and peace you need to ease your anxieties, strengthen your relationships, and encounter the almighty God during such trying times.

also available as eBooks

MOODY Publishers®

*From the Word to Life®*

encourages us to reset the rhythm of our days in light of God's sovereignty and strength. With anxiety on everyone's doorstep, we are all in need of soul salve, and these practical, poignant pages deliver!

**MATT HEARD**

Founder of THRIVE; author of *Life with a Capital L: Embracing Your God-Given Humanity*; and teaching pastor at Northland Church

*Psalms for the Anxious Heart* is tenderly and truthfully written to provide its readers with grace to feel understood in their moments of anxiety rather than feel judged. Becky Harling beautifully unpacks the poetry of the Psalms and brings powerful application as she shares vulnerable moments from her own life. There are no cliché answers or quick-fix suggestions offered; rather, Becky shares from a deep well of trusting the Lord through some of life's more difficult challenges. This devotional is beautifully inspiring and offers an anchor of hope through troubling times.

**STEPHANIE HENDERSON**

Executive Pastor, Women's Ministry and Guest Services, New Life Church

As I opened *Psalms for the Anxious Heart*, I wondered, "Can there be rich spiritual depth in such small daily portions?" The answer is a resounding YES! You will find hope in times of hopelessness, learn to lament in Day 5, and love the four daily sections to go deeper: "Selah," "Today's Truth," "Listen," and "Pray." Expect to find your soul enlarged. Mine was!

**LINDA DILLOW**

Bestselling author of *Calm My Anxious Heart* and *Satisfy My Thirsty Soul*

# Praise for *Psalms for the Anxious Heart*

Uncertain times often come our way. In *Psalms for the Anxious Heart*, Becky Harling shares the lessons she's learned through difficult days, as well as encouragement backed by Scripture. As she's discovered, when we take our anxious hearts to Jesus, we find an unexplainable peace and joy that will carry us through even the darkest moments.

**MICHELLE COX**
Bestselling author of *Just 18 Summers* and the *When God Calls the Heart* series

Every generation in history has faced insurmountable challenges—wars, economic instability, persecution, political unrest, devastation due to ferocious weather, and personal challenges. Each gives us a reason to wrestle with anxiety. There is no better place to go than to the Psalms for peace in the midst of every storm in life, and there is no wiser person to lead us into the refuge of His presence than Becky Harling. I don't know what you are dealing with today, but I can assure you that you will find Him in the Psalms and in the writings of my dear friend Becky.

**CAROL McLEOD**
Bible teacher and bestselling author of *Significant, StormProof,* and other titles

Some books are for information and others are for inspiration. *Psalms for the Anxious Heart* merges both of those into something deeper: an invitation. Becky Harling, speaking from her lifelong immersion in the Psalms, as well as an authentic engagement with her own story, issues a timely and compelling invitation to all of us living in the shadow of a global pandemic. Delving into the psalmists' recurring choices of praise over panic, she